Introducing
PRINCE

The Structured Project Management Method

C. Bentley

NCC Blackwell
MANCHESTER · OXFORD

British Library Cataloguing in Publication Data

Bentley, Colin
    Introducing PRINCE.
    I. Title
    005.1
    ISBN 1-85554-170-X

First published in 1992 by:

NCC Blackwell Limited, 108 Cowley Road, Oxford OX4 1JF, England.

Reprinted 1993.

Editorial Office, The National Computing Centre Limited, Oxford Road, Manchester M1 7ED, England.

Typeset in 10pt Times Roman by H & H Graphics, Blackburn; and printed by Hobbs the Printers Ltd, Southampton, SO9 2UZ.

ISBN 1-85554-170-X

Preface

The impact of poorly managed change programmes and projects is a source of major concern to all sizes and types of organisation. The impact can be seen in missed deadlines, escalating costs, poor quality end products. The root problems are likely to be:

- unclear objectives;

- poor communications within the project, and between project management, client and management;

- vague or non-existent plans. Plans not in sufficient detail;

- inadequate monitoring and control of actual work done. A failure at an early point to recognize that a deviation has occured from the expected schedule, budget or objectives;

- failure to control a change to specification once it has been agreed;

- poor or non-existent verification of the quality of the project's products as they are being delivered throughout the project.

Because of these experiences, there is increasing recognition that Project Management disciplines are an essential ingredient of modern business practice. This leads on to two further points.

1 Wouldn't it be sensible to have a standard Project Management Method which could apply to all the different types of project run by an organisation? This would mean that as staff moved from one project to another, they would be aware of the roles, procedures, processes and reporting formats. Training in the method could be standardised.

2 Why re-invent this particular wheel? There is possibly a Project Management Method already in existence which would suit our needs. If so, that method will already be documented. There will be training courses available in the method. It will have been proven over many projects, refined over years of practical experience.

The government went through such a thinking process in the 1970s. At that time, it was only thinking of IT projects, which badly needed a Project Management Method. The CCTA came up with PROMPT II as its choice, and this became the government standard for IT projects in 1979. This had really been designed with large projects in mind, and later it was felt that the method needed more flexibility in addressing smaller projects.

The result of their experiences and extra requirements was a series of modifications to PROMPT II, resulting in the creation of PRINCE. This is an acronym for PRojects IN Controlled Environments. The government is now pressing for the spread of the method from IT development to other types of project.

It is a very flexible method, suitable to many shapes and sizes of project. Its particular strengths are:

- definition of the roles which are needed in a project;

- involvement of the user at all levels in all aspects of the project from beginning to end;

- a comprehensive set of plans and controls relevant to the size and risk involved in the project;

- insistence on establishing that there is a viable business case for the project before any major expenditure is undertaken, and checking this at identified moments during the project.

For those faced with a need for a Project Management Method, or with a specific need to understand what PRINCE is all about, this book sets out the fundamentals and shows how they fit together into a compact method which can be used to solve the problems listed at the beginning of this preface. It is easy-to-read, using minimum jargon, and explaining any PRINCE terminology used.

Contents

1

Introduction

1.1 Project problems

There are numerous definitions of a project. It can be regarded as a series of activities carried out to achieve one or more objectives. It will be unique in some respect. It will have a defined start and end point, although the latter may be hard to find if it is a poorly managed project.

A few years ago I was asked to propose a project management method to the computer department of a large international company. They had drawn up a list of six typical complaints from their users:

- The end-product was not what we originally asked for.

- The system and the project changed direction without our realising it.

- The costs escalated without our realising it, then it was too late to stop it.

- We were told the system would be delivered late, but we were only told this when it was too late for us or the computer department to supply extra effort.

- We were in the dark during most of the development, and even now we do not really understand how to make the system work.

- The programs are not reliable, hence maintenance costs are more than we expected.

This was an embarrassing list for them, showing that the users were ignored during most of the project. This was apart from poor planning and control.

Speaking of control, the Hoskyns Group did a survey of projects some years ago and listed symptoms which they found to indicate projects which were out of control:

- direction unclear;

- over- or under-worked staff;

- people and things not here when needed;

- examples of rework or wasted effort;

- the last tasks were rushed;

- poor quality work;

- projects late and overspent;

- small problems had a big impact.

You might recognise some of the symptoms. But why do these problems occur? Their causes are the reasons why a formal project management method is needed:

- lack of user involvement;
- lack of co-ordination;
- lack of communication;
- inadequate planning;
- lack of progress control;
- lack of quality control;
- insufficient measurables.

So there we have it. Without good project management, projects will:

- take more time than expected;
- cost more than expected;
- deliver a product which is not exactly what the user wants;
- deliver a product of inadequate quality;
- not reveal their exact status until they finish.

There are other reasons for having the same formal project management method for all projects. It identifies the training which should be given to your project managers. It offers a consistency to higher management. They know what to expect, what to look for. Plans and reports are standardised. Project management methods are based on the experience of many people and many projects. Therefore, they will contain all general needs and steer the project manager away from many of the common mistakes. These common mistakes are most likely to recur when people are running a project for the first time. They need a project management method to help them avoid all the problems highlighted above.

1.2   Why a method of project management is necessary

Figure 1.1 gives an idea of the elements of a project which make a project management method essential. A project means a job to be done within certain constraints to a required specification. Various products will have to be produced, and these will require activities which take time and resources. These will need to be planned to make sure that the target can be achieved within the constraints. Once under way, there must be controls to ensure that the project keeps to the plan. There will be a need for techniques, some for the technical activities, others to help create the plan and maintain control. Monitoring and ensuring the quality of the products will also need techniques. There are many types of resource which will be consumed. People will be one of the most important resources and a method of organising, co-ordinating and directing them will be needed. All of these things are found in a project management method.

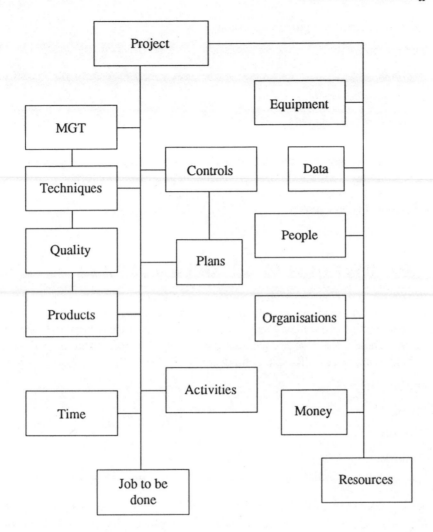

Figure 1.1 Project elements

1.3 What PRINCE has to offer

The acronym, PRINCE, stands for:

PRojects IN Controlled Environments

PRINCE is a structured method for the effective project management of IT projects. It is the standard method for use in government departments. The original method was PROMPT II, developed in the 70s, aimed at large projects. The CCTA has made major enhancements to the original and renamed it PRINCE. One improvement was to make it comply with BS 5750, the quality systems standard.

The success criteria for a project are to complete:-

– on time;

– within budget;

– to the specified quality;

– a product of the required specification.

The achievement of these criteria needs a method, an approach which will work time and time again for projects of any size. PRINCE helps do this by ensuring at the start that everyone involved knows where the project is going, what the steps are to get there, and who is to do what. It then provides checks at key moments to ensure the four targets are being achieved - time, budget, functionality and quality.

1.4   An overview of a PRINCE project

PRINCE provides a flexible project framework, a set of structures and techniques. It defines an organisation structure for a project, the structure and content of project plans, and a set of controls and reports which monitor whether the project is proceeding to plan, and ensure reaction to deviations. These three, together with the products of the project and the activities which produce them, comprise the PRINCE components:

– Organisation;

– Plans;

– Controls;

– Products;

– Activities.

Unlike any other project management method, PRINCE revolves around the products which are to be produced by the project. Identification of the products tells you what activities will be needed to create them. These activities then trigger off the planning sequence, define the quality measurements and activities, and indicate the timings for the various controls.

1.4.1   IT Strategy and PRINCE

Although it concentrates on project management, PRINCE does set out the relationship with IT Strategy and business planning. Figure 1.2 shows this. Those responsible for IT strategy have to consider what IT environment and what systems will best fit with the business strategy over the next, say, ten years. This includes central or distributed processing, central or distributed data, decisions on compatible hardware, operating systems, database languages, teleprocessing software, full-time staff or contractors, as well as what systems are needed. There will be many options facing the IT strategy group in all these areas. In order to make a choice of where best to spend their limited resources, the group will have a number of studies undertaken.

In computer project jargon, these studies will comprise problem definition and feasibility

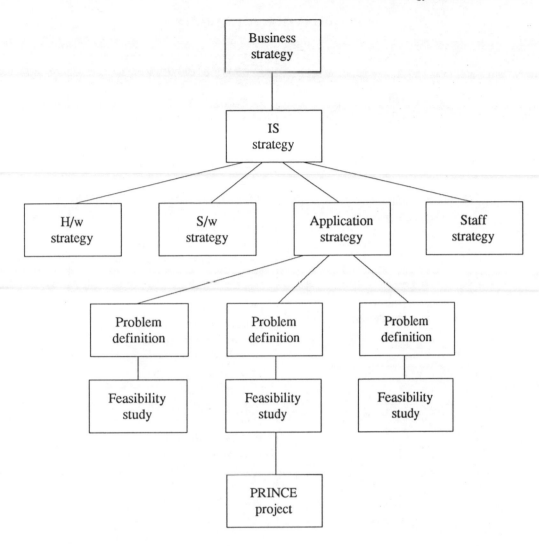

Figure 1.2 Business and IT strategy

study. Based upon the results of these studies, the IT strategy group will decide to undertake certain projects.

The organisation to handle this is seen in Figure 1.3. The IS Steering Committee is the liaison with business planning, looking five to ten years ahead on the systems environment, hardware, software and information systems which will be needed. The committee commission studies into possible options open to them in order to implement their strategy. The selected options are prioritised and passed down to the IT Executive Committee. Here resources are allocated, the project board and project manager roles are identified, and a project brief handed over. The project board then take over responsibility for the project until its conclusion.

ORGANISATION HIERARCHY

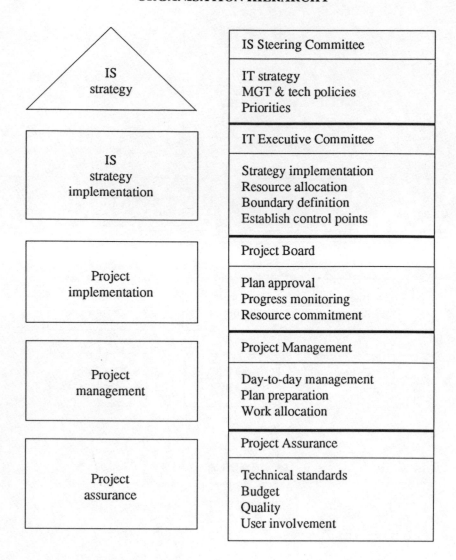

Figure 1.3   IT strategy and PRINCE

1.4.2 The Organisation Component

Figure 1.4 identifies some of the different aspects of a project manager's job. The project manager should be aware of the IT strategy of the company and able to talk to someone about project decisions which have an external impact. There is liaison with the client and his or her own line management, and negotiations about funding for the project. The project manager is also responsible for planning, monitoring against that plan and checking quality and conformity with standards. There are constant changes to needs, and calls to know the status of one product

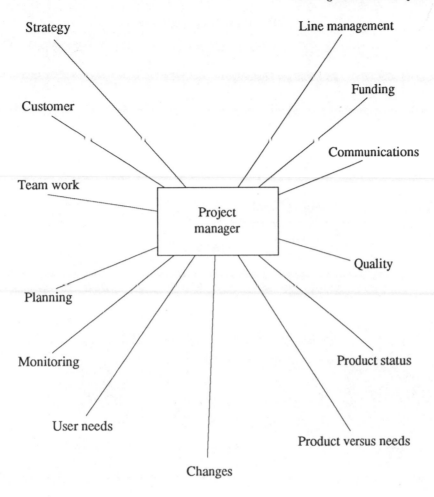

Figure 1.4 Project manager concerns

or another. The project doesn't have to be very big before the project manager does not have the time to be on top of all of these things. Unless, that is, there is an organisation structure to show to whom the project manager can go for guidance, to whom some of these jobs can be delegated.

Figure 1.5 shows the PRINCE organisation. The organisation structure identifies project roles, the experience and training needed, lines of authority, reporting and communication. It defines the responsibilities of the user and higher management, how and when they are involved as well as the roles of the project team. It describes how the user keeps in close touch on a day-to-day basis with the entire development.

Within PRINCE, responsibilities are defined in terms of roles, rather than individuals. Assignment of roles to individuals is a decision for each project to take according to its size, how many user areas are involved and the availability of resources. The same individual may be assigned to more than one role, to different roles at different stages of the project, or a role may be shared by more than one person.

PRINCE ORGANISATION

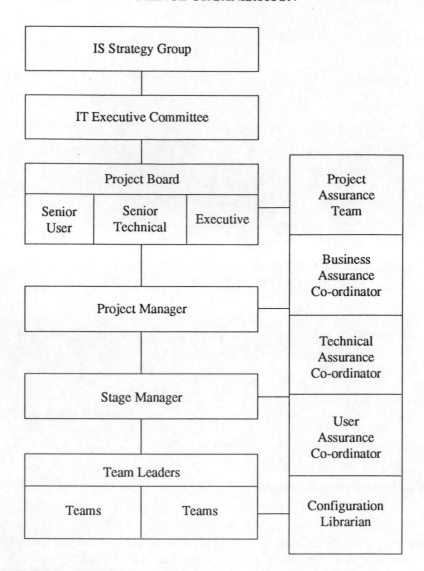

Figure 1.5   Prince organisation

1.4.2.1   The Project Board

The Project Board is appointed by the IT Executive Committee to take overall control of a PRINCE project. It consists of three senior management roles, each representing major project interests.

- Executive, the formal reporting line to the IT Executive Committee, who ensures that the project's objectives and constraints are being met, and provides overall project guidance and assessment throughout.

- Senior User, representing users of the final system.

- Senior Technical, representing the resources which have responsibility for technical implementation.

1.4.2.2 Project Manager

The Project Manager has day-to-day responsibility for management of the project from beginning to end.

1.4.2.3 The Stage Manager

In a large or complex project, the Project Manager may need to delegate some work. One or more Stage Manager roles may be assigned the responsibility to ensure that the products of particular stages or sub-stages are produced. Depending on the resources required and/or skills available, the Project Board may choose to appoint:

- one Project Manager who also assumes the role of Stage Manager throughout;

- one Project Manager, supported by a Stage Manager for each stage. For example, a stage in which requirements are specified might have a stage manager appointed from the user community, then a stage manager from the IS group to look after development and finally a user to stage manage the installation. These would all report to the project manager to provide continuity. In another scenario, there might be a need to be simultaneously doing jobs requiring different expertise. A project manager could have three stage managers at the same time, one for the construction of a computer room, a second developing software and a third looking after the collection and cleaning of data;

- a succession of Stage Managers, each assuming the role of Project Manager for the duration of the stage.

1.4.2.4 Stage Teams

For each stage there is a team responsible for producing the products of that stage. There may even be a need for several teams within a stage. The team composition may change from one stage to another, reflecting the skills and knowledge required. The team organisation and responsibility definitions will depend upon the size and nature of the project and the skill mix available. PRINCE recognises the need to establish Team Leader roles where appropriate.

1.4.2.5 The Project Assurance Team

The Project Assurance Team (PAT) is a grouping of expertise to help and advise the project and to provide a level of independent monitoring of the project on behalf of the user and any standards and/or quality assurance group. This expertise covers planning and costing, quality control, relevant technical standards, knowledge of the specific user area(s), and product control. The team consists of:

- Business Assurance Co-ordinator (BAC), to maintain administrative controls against schedules and budget, and also play a leading role in quality control;

- Technical Assurance Co-ordinator (TAC), to advise on standards and techniques, monitor and report on the technical quality of the work;

- User Assurance Co-ordinator (UAC), to provide input on user needs and represent the users' interests;

- Configuration Librarian (CL), to maintain the files of all the technical, management and quality documents and products.

1.4.3   The Products Component

A cornerstone of PRINCE is the definition of the products to be produced by the project. From this comes identification of the quality criteria for each product, the activities required to generate the products, and the sequencing of these activities.

PRINCE divides consideration of products into three:

- management;

- technical;

- quality.

Management products are all the contracts, plans, approvals of them and reports against them. Quality products cover all the definitions of quality criteria, product reviews and all the documents leading from the reviews. The technical products required by the end user should be identified in the Project Brief by the Project Board. Additional technical products may be defined by the technical strategy which is appropriate to a particular stage.

1.4.4   The Activities Component

Management activities are concerned with planning, monitoring and reporting the work of the project and with acquiring the various approvals and agreements. They produce management products in the form of plans, reports and other control documents.

The technical activities undertaken by a project are determined entirely by the scope and objectives of the project. They describe the work needed to produce the products required from the project.

Quality activities cover all the product reviews and testing.

1.4.5   The Plans Component

Planning and replanning are key activities of managing any project. There are four levels of planning in PRINCE, shown in Figure 1.6. Plans are prepared for the project as a whole, for each stage, sometimes for a complex activity within a stage and for each individual's work within the stage. At each level, PRINCE addresses the need for technical planning, resource planning and quality planning.

Technical Plans are concerned with the products to be delivered and with the activities necessary to ensure that the products emerge on time and to the required quality standards.

Resource Plans summarise the resources and budget needed by the project. They are derived from the corresponding Technical Plan.

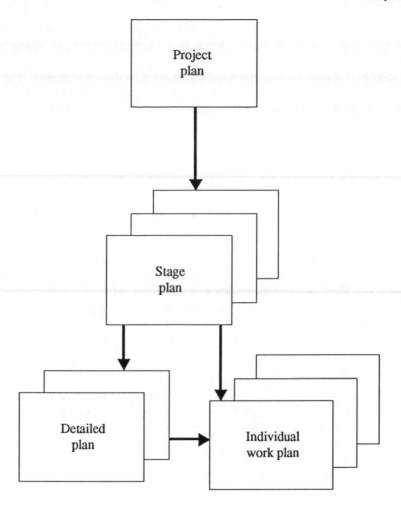

Figure 1.6 PRINCE planning levels

Quality plans cover the action which must be taken to ensure that the project can deliver products of the desired quality. Quality criteria must be defined and agreed, and a testing strategy adopted. Quality Review procedures must be established, and review activities must be defined and resourced.

The resulting quality planning activities must be integrated into the Technical Plan at each level. Just as quality must be built into the products, so must quality control be built into the plans.

1.4.5.1 Project Plans

The Project Technical Plan is created at the very beginning of a project. It charts the major activities of the project. It is used with the Project Resource Plan to provide an estimate of total time and costs before heavy expenditure begins, and then to monitor progress on the project as a whole. It addresses strategic issues related to Quality Control and Configuration Management.

The Project Resource Plan identifies the type, amount and cost of the resources required by the entire project. The purpose is to help the Project Board view the viability of the project before major expense is incurred.

The Project Quality Plan sets the overall quality strategy for the entire project. It defines the standards to be followed and the quality criteria for the major products. It also identifies external constraints, eg a specific Configuration Management Method.

1.4.5.2   Stage Plans

A Stage Technical Plan shows the products, activities and quality controls for one stage of the project. It represents a commitment from the Project Manager to the Project Board. The Stage Technical Plan is produced and approved at the end of the previous stage, the plan for the first stage having been prepared during project initiation.

A Stage Resource Plan summarises the resources required by a particular stage. It defines the budget required by the stage and is used to report actual expenditure and resource usage against plan.

A Stage Quality Plan identifies the quality criteria, test methods and review guidelines for each product produced during the stage. Activities are defined and resources allocated for quality reviews and approval of test specifications and results.

1.4.5.3   Detailed Plans

Detailed Technical Plans will exist in some projects, to give a further breakdown of particular major activities, eg system testing, data gathering, cleaning and conversion. Figure 1.7 shows how a Detailed Technical Plan might be used. The resources and budget will be summarised in a Detailed Resource Plan and any quality work will be added into the Detailed Technical Plan in a similar manner to the Stage Plan.

1.4.5.4   Individual Work Plans

Individual Work Plans are derived from the Stage and Detailed Technical Plans and allocate detailed activities to members of a stage team. They should be accompanied by a product description of the required item(s).

1.4.5.5   Tolerance

However carefully a plan is made, the actual performance will not match it exactly. For this reason a safety margin is agreed. This is a margin above and below the lines on a graph showing the accumulating cost and time of a plan. The actual performance is allowed to fluctuate within these margins and still be considered under control. This safety margin is called the tolerance level.

The IT Executive Committee should hand down to the Project Board a tolerance level guide for the project. The project manager has to agree a tolerance level for each stage plan with the Project Board. Apart from the overall guidelines, the amount of tolerance (usually expressed as a percentage) will be influenced by the project manager's feeling of confidence. Has such a plan

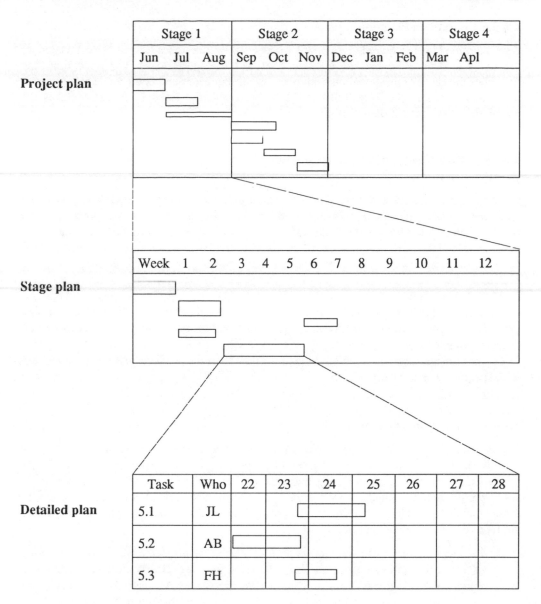

Figure 1.7 Detailed plan

been tackled before? Is the performance of the resources reliable? How many unknowns lie ahead?

It is common practice to have the same percentage tolerance for budget and schedule, but this may not be the best idea. Has the user different priorities for budget and schedule? Might the unknown factors ahead be more likely to affect one rather than the other?

So the stage tolerance level defines a safety margin within which the stage costs and time can deviate without further reference to the Project Board.

1.4.5.6   Exception Planning

An Exception Plan is required in situations where costs or timescales have already deviated, or are likely to deviate, beyond the tolerances set by the Project Board. The Exception Plan describes the cause of the deviation from plan, its consequences and options and recommends corrective action to the Project Board. Once approved, the Exception Plan replaces the remainder of the current Stage Plan.

1.4.6   The Controls Component

Regular and formal monitoring of actual progress against plan is essential to ensure the timeliness, cost control and quality of the system under development. PRINCE provides a structure of management and product-oriented controls to monitor progress, supported by a reporting procedure which enables replanning or other corrective action to be taken. Figure 1.8 gives an idea of the PRINCE controls. All the controls involve monitoring a situation, detecting errors or deviations, reporting on the situation found and triggering any necessary corrective action.

There are two concerns: business and technical. On the business side, schedule and cost are the two main items to be controlled. But at specified times there is a check on the continuing presence of a good business case for the project. This includes verifying that the risks remain at an acceptable level.

On the technical side, there are controls of the quality of the products and their comparison with specified requirements.

1.4.6.1   Management Controls

These controls cover all aspects of project activity and, at the highest level, allow senior management to assess project status prior to committing further expenditure. Controls are applied via meetings of project management and project staff, with each meeting producing a set of pre-defined documents. Management Controls must be defined at Project Initiation to ensure that the project has clear terms of reference and an adequate management structure. There are five key management controls:

- *Project Initiation*   This provides a positive start to the project, ensuring that the terms of reference, objectives, plans and job definitions are clearly defined, published, understood and agreed. The project plan and business case have assured the Project Board that the project is worthwhile and should show an acceptable return on investment.

- *End Stage Assessment (ESA)*   This is a mandatory management control and occurs at the end of each stage. It consists of a formal presentation to the Project Board by the project (and stage) manager of the current project status. It also requests approval of the Resource and Technical Plans for the next stage. Project Board approval must be obtained before the project can proceed in other than a limited way (see MSA) to the next stage.

- *Mid Stage Assessment (MSA)*   This may be held to introduce a review part-way through a long stage; to authorise limited work to begin on the next stage before the current stage is complete; or to review an Exception Plan when the project has deviated from the original plans.

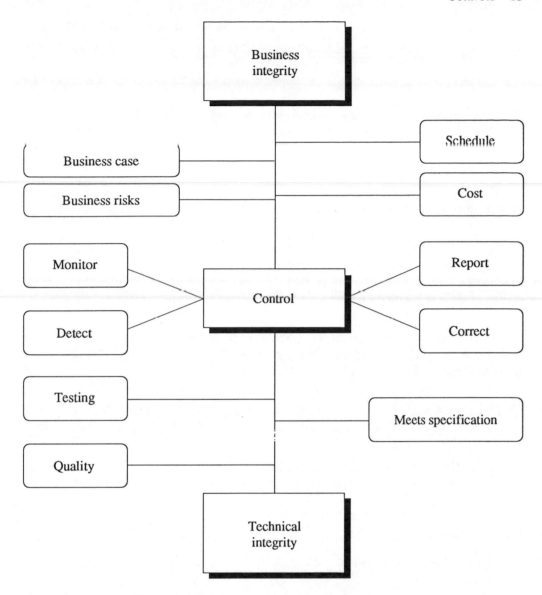

Figure 1.8   Prince control approach

- *Checkpoint Meeting*   These are conducted regularly with the stage team by the stage manager or on his behalf by the Project Assurance Team. They provide the basic progress information used to measure actual achievement against plan on both Stage Technical and Resource Plans

- *Highlight Report*   Information is gathered from the checkpoint Reports and summarised by the project manager for the Project Board on a regular, agreed basis.

– *Project Closure*   A review of the project's work is held when it finishes. This is to examine how successful it was in producing the required products and also if any lessons could be learned to improve future projects.

1.4.6.2   Product Controls

Quality and technical controls are applied to specific products rather than to the overall output of a stage or project. The aim is to identify and correct errors as early as possible in the development process.

Quality Review   At each Quality Review, appropriate technical and user staff examine a product to ensure that it is complete and meets its quality criteria and user requirements.

Product Descriptions   Before being created, each product is described: why it is needed, what its composition will be and how its final quality will be assessed. The description is not only given to the team member who will create it, but also to those who later come to review the quality of the finished product.

Technical Exceptions   A Technical Exception is an unplanned change relating to one or more products. It needs to be recorded and action agreed in order to prevent uncontrolled divergence from plans.

Configuration Management   Configuration Management is the control of all products to be produced by the project. A Configuration Management Method (CMM) provides a formal mechanism for:

– identifying and labelling required products;

– tracking their development status;

– recording the relationships between them;

– controlling the submission of these products to appropriate libraries;

– controlling access to them.

2
Getting off to a controlled start

2.1 Project Initiation

Project Initiation is getting a project off to a formal start, with everyone knowing their role, agreeing what job is to be done, confirming that there are good business reasons for doing it, and ensuring that any risks involved have been assessed. A feasibility study may or may not have already been done as part of the IS strategy work, but a PRINCE project must start off with this initiation step.

The product coming out of it is the Project Initiation Document, containing:

- Terms of reference;
- Acceptance criteria;
- Project organisation structure;
- Business case;
- Business risk assessment;
- Business risk proposals;
- Project plan;
- Project quality plan;
- Configuration management plan;
- Stage selection;
- First stage plan;
- First stage quality plan.

In its appendices there will be:

- Job descriptions
- Product descriptions
- Project plan working documents
- Stage plan working documents

When the document has been produced there must be a meeting between the project manager and the Project Board. It is recommended that the project assurance team also attends, together

17

with the stage manager of the first stage, if this role is to be used. This is an important meeting as it is the official start point of the project. Here is a description of that meeting.

2.1.1 The Project Initiation Meeting

Purpose
  – Formal initiation of the project.

Timing
  – At or near the project start.

Agenda
  – Agree project terms of reference, scope and constraints
  – Confirm the business justification
    • is there an adequate business case, what are the likely business risks, what proposals are there where a serious business risk exists?
  – Confirm organisation, appointments and responsibilities
    • project board, project and stage management, project assurance team
  – Approve project plans
  – Approve first stage plan
  – Define controls
    • quality plans, technical exceptions, configuration management method
  – Determine tolerance level for first stage
    • budget, schedule, deviation procedure
  – Decide reporting requirements
    • levels, frequencies, content, problem procedure

2.2   Setting up the Project Organisation

The Project Board should have been appointed by the IT Executive Committee. As part of project initiation their roles and responsibilities are defined, plus all the other management and assurance team roles.

2.3   Creating a Project Plan

Chapter 6 describes the planning steps in detail. The purpose of the project plan is to give the Project Board an idea of the total cost and time of the project before they commit to large expenditure on it. The estimated costs from the project plan also go into the business case to find out if there will be an acceptable return on the investment.

The project plan will not be in fine detail. In a project lasting six months to a year, the plan might identify ten to twenty products needed on the way to the final system, each product taking weeks to produce. It should be possible to see the entire technical plan on one page. If it is in too much detail, spreading over several pages, it will be difficult to understand and will have taken too long to produce. The aim of initiation is to quickly and cheaply get an idea of whether the job can and should be done.

2.4   Defining the Project Quality Plan

As described in the introduction, at the project level the plan text should point to the quality methods and standards to be used, the major products to be checked and how the quality work can be verified. Perhaps the best way of illustrating this is to give an example of what might be written:

'1   The quality control methods to be used in this project are based on British Standard BS5750. A quality file has been opened which will contain details of all the quality control work carried out and the results of that work.

2   In Appendix 1 are descriptions of the major products of the project. For quality control purposes these contain details of the expected composition of the product, the quality criteria to be applied to it and the method of assessing the quality.

3   All the key products will be subjected to a quality review by the team with participation from the User Assurance Co-ordinator. All other products will be put through informal reviews.

4   All quality review documentation and results will be filed and monitored by the Business Assurance Co-ordinator and will be open for inspection by the User Assurance Co-ordinator and client quality assurance personnel.

5   Prior to its release the total product will undergo system testing and user acceptance testing to check on the software, procedures and usability of the system.'

2.5   Product Descriptions

As part of quality control, PRINCE requires a description to be written out for a product before that product is made. This ensures that we have thought about what is needed before diving in, the person to whom the product is allocated has a good definition of what is needed, and there is something against which the end product can be measured. The contents of a product description are:

- Title of the product;

- Purpose;

- Composition;

- Form or format;

- Derivation;

- External dependencies;

- Quality criteria;

- Quality measurement method.

For standard IT projects, PRINCE offers descriptions of the normal products.

2.6   Configuration Management

As part of the project plan there should be a statement of how the products will be controlled as they are finished. Who will be in charge of ensuring that the latest version of a product will be used, that obsolete copies of products will be withdrawn, that untested programs don't get into an operational system? Will there be a product identification system? What libraries will be used? Where will things be kept? Will there be any security to control access and modification to products? Can we keep track of products? Will we know who is working on a product, who has copies? All of these activities are controlled by the Configuration Librarian role. The chosen Configuration Management Method must be identified in the plan text of the project plan with a cross-reference to who will be carrying out the role.

2.7   Stage Selection

Trying to plan a complete project in detail is very difficult. The bigger or more complex the project, the more difficult it is. You can spend too long in planning, and the end is so far ahead there are too many guesses and unknowns. This is the view of the planner. If you look from the clients' point of view, they would say they want to know in advance to what they are committing. They would want to be able to stop the project if it were going wrong. Either party might want part payments to be matched to reaching a certain point satisfactorily.

The overall idea is this: a project plan is needed to give both Project Board and project manager an idea of what the total time, cost and resource need is going to be. This plan is needed quickly and we don't want its production to be expensive. When the project plan has been made, the Project Board and project manager look at it and decide into what stages it should be broken. The actual commitment they make is to the first stage plan, not the project plan. The project manager has to feel comfortable that the stage can be planned in detail. This means that activities can be broken down until they need just a few days, say ten days maximum. Also actual resources can be identified for each activity. The Project Board has to feel happy about committing the budget for the stage plan.

Towards the end of the first stage, the project manager prepares the next stage plan. It's now much closer in time, the experience of the first stage has been gained, there will be fewer unknowns. In considering whether to accept the next plan, the Project Board view the accuracy of the first stage plan and compare the new plan to that part of the project plan which it covers. And so it moves forward from one stage to the next.

Most project management methods offer a fixed set of stages and you have to fit your project into their idea of stages. PRINCE is much more flexible than this. You look at the project plan and choose what stages are suitable based on the products being available.

So there we have it. PRINCE stage selection is based on the the size of the project, how far ahead can be comfortably seen, the risks involved, the key decisions which have to be made and coincides with the delivery of the major products of the project throughout the development cycle.

2.8 A Stage Plan

As described above, the stages will have been chosen by examination of the project plan. The products due to be produced in the first stage, according to the project plan, are taken as the basis and broken down into finer detail. The planning sequence is exactly the same as for the project plan, described in detail in Chapter 6.

At a project level it is acceptable to identify just the number and type of resource required to produce a product, but at stage level the required resource must be identified by name against each activity and the work effort shown against the timeframe.

2.9 The Stage Quality Plan

There are two parts to a stage quality plan. The Stage Technical Plan will show the planned quality review activities and the resources allocated to them. Any testing activities will also be in the plan. In the plan text will be confirmation of the stage products to be reviewed, including any informal ones which may not be shown separately in the plan. It is worth pointing out, for the peace of mind of the Senior User, where the User Assurance Co-ordinator is to be involved in the quality reviews. Any change of quality responsibilities should be described.

3
Keeping Control

Once a stage has begun, PRINCE offers a number of methods and reports to ensure that the project and stage managers and the project assurance team keep control of progress. These controls contain reports to the Project Board which give them confidence that things are under control.

3.1   Checkpoint reports

A checkpoint is a regular meeting of the project team to report on and review the technical status of the stage work. It usually occurs weekly. The frequency is decided by the project manager and identified in the stage plan. The checkpoint meeting is normally conducted by the team leader. If the team leader is absent, the Technical or Business Assurance Co-ordinator may stand in. The aims of a checkpoint are to ensure that all team members are aware of what the others are doing, especially in areas which impact their work, and report back to the stage manager (or project manager if the stage manager role is not used). A useful checklist of questions for each member is:

What have I done since the previous meeting?

What do I intend doing next?

Have I any problems?

Have I had any problems?

Do I anticipate any problems?

Have I come across any information useful to others?

The opportunity is also taken to refresh individual work plans where necessary and pass news from other teams or project level or more general information down to the team. The checkpoint report is informal, but it is recommended by the author that it has three sections: achievements this period, achievements next period, problems (current and potential).

3.2   Highlight reports

The highlight report is sent by the project manager to the Project Board on a frequency agreed at the previous end stage assessment or project initiation meeting. A bi-monthly frequency is normal. It is a summary of the checkpoint reports under three headings: achievements this period, problems (current or potential) and achievements next period. A sample of what the report might look like is in Appendix 1. It is recommended that the report is limited normally to one page. This gives it the best chance of being read quickly by the Project Board members and highlights the essential information.

When the highlight report is sent to the Project Board, it is accompanied by updated stage technical and resource plans.

3.3   Quality reviews

A quality review is the most important technical control in PRINCE. It assesses the quality of an individual product after any step in its lifecycle, allowing very early error trapping. A file is kept of all the quality review process: the invitations, attendees, results, corrective actions and sign-offs. This is an important part of conforming to PRINCE, because it provides an audit trail of the quality checking which is being done, and can be inspected by the user or an independent quality assurance group at any time.

A quality review is an examination by one or more people of another person's product in a face-to-face meeting. The full quality review procedure is described in Chapter 6.

The aim of a quality review is to find any errors, deviations from standards or omissions in a product once its author claims it is finished. In order to keep the review meeting within a limit of two hours, it may be only a part product which is reviewed.

A quality review has three phases: preparation, review and follow-up. There are defined roles for participants and the review must appear in the stage technical plan. As an attendee, it is a major control and communication point where the User Assurance Co-ordinator can confirm that the project is producing what the user wants.

3.4   End stage assessment

The end stage assessment is a meeting between the Project Board, project manager and project assurance team. If the stage manager role is being used, the current and next stage managers would both be present. The objectives are to assess the performance of the stage which is just finishing, review the status of specification changes, review any changes to the business case, and approve the next stage plans. The timing is at (or close to) the end of each stage and before work starts on the next stage. This is the ideal but it may prove difficult to get everyone together at the exact moment.

A typical agenda for an end stage assessment would be:

– Project manager's report on the current stage

– Project assurance team's review of:

  • user assurance,

  • quality work,

  • project issue status,

  • standards;

- Re-assessment of the project plan;
- Business case review;
- Project manager's presentation of the next stage plan;
- Project plan impact of the next stage plan;
- Business case impact of the next stage plan;
- Project assurance team assessment of the next stage plan;
- Project Board decision.

The activities for the Project Board are to:

- review and agree the scope and objectives of the next stage;
- review the technical approach;
- review the planning assumptions made;
- review the plan risks;
- identify any management actions to remove or reduce those risks;
- set the plan tolerance level;
- approve the quality plan;
- decide whether to approve the plan or not.

4

Controlling change

In any project lasting more than half an hour, the requirements will change. No matter how well planned a project may be, if changes are not controlled, the project is likely to be a disaster, at least from the point of view of budget and schedule. It will also be difficult to agree that requirements have been met.

Requirements may not be the only changes during the life of a stage plan. Anything could go wrong or prove impossible to fulfil. For these reasons, all changes to a project must be carefully controlled.

4.1   Technical exceptions

A Technical Exception is an unplanned situation concerning one or more products. It covers a change to requirements, an additional need, a failure by a product to meet specification, an omission, or a failure for some event to occur when planned. There is a procedure to trap, monitor and control all of these.

4.1.1   Technical Exception Procedure Objectives

These are:

- to identify and deal with all situations which may prejudice the successful completion of the project or operation of the system;

- to ensure that the impact of all Technical Exceptions is assessed before a decision is made;

- to ensure that all work is viewed within agreed priorities;

- to ensure that all Technical Exceptions are monitored until an agreed decision is implemented;

- to provide a formal way of advising other projects of Technical Exceptions which might affect them.

4.1.2   Technical Exception Documents

All Technical Exceptions are first recorded on a Project Issue Report. They are assessed and may be transferred to a Request For Change or Off-Specification document.

4.1.2.1   Project Issue Report

An example of a Project Issue Report is shown in Appendix 1. It can be raised at any time by anyone about anything concerning the project. It is passed to the Configuration Librarian who logs it, passes a copy back to the originator, files a copy and sends the original to the Project Assurance Team.

The Project Assurance Team are responsible for evaluating the issue. The Technical Assurance Co-ordinator and Configuration Librarian identify what other products are affected and the effort involved, and this is costed out by the Business Assurance Co-ordinator. A regular meeting of stage manager and Project Assurance Team is held, the frequency of which depends on the number of Project Issues being submitted and the length of the stage. A normal frequency is weekly.

At the meeting, all outstanding Project Issue Reports are reviewed. If any can be fully answered without incurring extra work, this is done. The Project Issue Report is annotated, the original filed by the Configuration Librarian and a copy sent to the originator.

Otherwise, each one is discussed. It may be held back for further investigation, but the aim is to present the Project Issue Report to the project manager with a recommendation on action to take. Only the project manager can authorise work to be done.

If an error in a product is discovered during a Quality Review, this is entered on a Quality Review Action List, not a Project Issue Report. There are only two exceptions to this. If the error is in a different product from the one under review, then it is put onto a Project Issue Report. Secondly, if an item on the Quality Review Action List cannot be corrected within the time allocated, the review chairman may agree to transfer it to a Project Issue Report.

At the end of each stage the Project Board must be told the status of Project Issues. By the project closure, all Project Issue Reports have to be closed.

4.1.2.2   Request For Change

If the analysis of the Project Issue Report indicates that this is a change to requirements, the project manager can authorise its transfer to a Request For Change. A sample of what this might look like is in Appendix 1.

Having decided that it is a Request For Change does not automatically mean that it will be implemented. The Project Board has the choice of rejecting it, adopting it immediately or deferring the decision. The Senior User has the responsibility of prioritising the requests and making recommendations to the Project Board. If it is adopted, the project manager can go ahead immediately as long as the extra work can be done within the agreed tolerance level of the current stage plan. If it goes beyond that, the project manager must have an Exception Plan agreed by the Project Board before the Request For Change can be implemented.

Alternatively, it can be deferred to the next stage plan or even a later enhancement to the system once this project is closed.

Whatever decision is taken, the originator is informed at every change and the file kept up-to-date.

4.1.2.3   Off-Specification

This is used to document any way in which the system fails to meet its specification. A sample is shown in Appendix 1. As with Requests For Change, only the project manager can make the decision to convert a Project Issue Report into an Off- Specification Report. The same options exist. It can be corrected, deferred until a later stage or enhancement project, or left as an Off-Specification. If the latter course of action is chosen, the Project Board must be informed at the end stage assessment. If the decision is to correct it, it can be done within the current stage plan only if the resources and time required stay within the plan tolerance. Otherwise an Exception Plan is needed.

Because the Off-Specification affects one of the current products, it is filed with the product in the technical file.

4.2   Creating an exception plan

Each stage plan has an agreed tolerance level or 'corridor' within which the actual costs and time spent can vary. If the budget and/or schedule have deviated outside the tolerance level, or are about to do so, the project manager must meet with the Project Board and tell them. It may be that a resource has not performed up to the expected standard, activities were underestimated or forgotten, an external dependency has failed or is late, or that a change in requirements cannot be handled within the current plan. The project manager must create an Exception Plan and present it to the Project Board. This is done at a mid stage assessment.

An Exception Plan is like a mini stage plan. It consists of a technical plan, resource plan and quality plan. It covers the time from the present moment to the stage end and replaces the rest of the stage plan. In addition, it contains the following information:

- description of the exception and reasons for its occurrence;
- prediction of the cost, schedule and technical impact if no action is taken;
- recommended recovery action;
- consequences of the recovery action on stage and project;
- any new or different assumptions;
- any change to prerequisites or risks;
- impact on the Business Case:
  - if no action is taken,
  - of the recommended recovery action.

4.3   Mid stage assessments

This is very similar to an end stage assessment. It has the same attendees and its major purpose is to review and approve a new plan. There are three reasons for holding a mid stage assessment.

4.3.1 Deviation

The agenda for such a meeting would be:

Review of the stage so far;

Deviation and its reasons;

Forecast impact by stage and project end;

Options;

Project manager's recommendation;

Exception plan;

Project Assurance Team comments;

Project Board decision.

4.3.2   Early Start to the Next Stage

A second reason for a mid stage assessment can be to gain approval for a limited amount of work for the next stage before the end stage assessment of the current stage.

Officially, at one end stage assessment a project manager gets approval for the work contained in the next stage plan and no more. The Project Board will have a look at the stage's results before deciding whether to approve the next stage plan. It may be sensible to overlap some work of the next stage, based on products already completed and approved. It would ruin the whole concept of control by the Project Board if the project manager could just begin such work without the approval (or even the knowledge) of the board.

So for any such overlapping work, the project manager must produce a mini stage plan, covering the amount of work to be done before the formal end stage assessment, and ask for Project Board approval for it. The mid stage assessment here has a very similar agenda to the end stage assessment, except that the current stage report will be incomplete.

4.3.3   Confidence Boost

One of the reasons for an end stage assessment is to ensure that the user feels in control at regular points throughout the project. If a stage is long, this feeling of control can waver. It is recommended in long stages (say, over ten weeks) that there is a mid stage assessment every six to eight weeks. This is a face-to-face report from the project and stage managers and Project Assurance Team to the Project Board. It has the same agenda as the end stage assessment, omitting the next stage plan.

5

Ending a project

5.1   Project evaluation report

The project evaluation report is completed by the project manager as input to the project closure. It is the project manager's assessment of how the project went. Its content is:

- *Performance* Achievements versus objectives. This is a checklist against the original project objectives and acceptance criteria. Have they been achieved or not?

  Actual versus planned expense. A review against the original project plan and reasons for any deviation.

- *Productivity* Compared to similar projects, how efficient was it? Was there any waste time, lost time?

- *Quality* How many technical exceptions were raised? A summary of them by stage, showing their criticality. Quality review statistics - how many done, results and so on.

- *Development method review* Were new methods used? What were the results of using them - benefits, problems? Can they be recommended?

- *Project management review* Did the project conform to project management standards? Are there any lessons to be learned?

5.2   Acceptance letters

There are five acceptance letters produced near the end of a project.

5.2.1   System Acceptance Letter

After system test the Senior Technical member of the Project Board, representing the line management of the development team, writes this letter, stating that to the best knowledge of the project the product is ready for installation.

5.2.2   User Acceptance Letter

After any acceptance tests this letter is written by the Senior User member of the Project Board, stating that the user is prepared to accept the system into production.

5.2.3   Operations Acceptance Letter

At the same time, assuming that they have been involved in any acceptance tests, the Operations Manager must prepare for the signature of the Senior User a letter stating that operations are prepared to accept the system into production.

5.2.4   Business Acceptance Letter

After the formal project closure the Executive of the Project Board has to write this letter to the IT Executive Committee, stating whether the project's objectives were met.

5.2.5   Security Acceptance Letter

If required, this is signed by the Executive on closure of the project. It confirms that any necessary security requirements of the operational project have been met.

5.3   Project closure

At the end of the project there is a meeting similar to an end stage assessment. The aim is to avoid the project dribbling on and confusion arising between where the original project ends and maintenance and enhancement begin.

Project closure is like a final end stage assessment, a meeting between Project Board, project manager and assurance team. The project evaluation report is input to the meeting. The job of the meeting is to:

- check that all products are complete and delivered;

- check that the status of any outstanding off-specifications and requests for change have been documented;

- check that all project issues have been cleared;

- approve the project evaluation report;

- arrange for the post implementation review.

5.4   Post implementation review

A post implementation review is carried out when the system has settled down, is running with its full load, and its performance has been tuned. This review can be some time after the project has ended, maybe months later.

The review is a comparison of the implementation and actual results of the project against the project brief. Officially, it is prepared by the Executive of the Project Board for the IT Executive Committee, but so many detailed statistics are expected that the Executive will delegate a lot of the work. The content of the report from the review is:

- file sizes and file growth. These figures are to check if the original ideas about the system size were justified;

- manpower needs. The cost/benefit case made certain assumptions about how much the operation of the new system would cost. This helps identify the accuracy of that claim;

- turn-round and response times. Has the system lived up to the performance criteria?

- error rates. What is the quality of the system. How does this reflect on the quality work done during the project?

- security;

- problems and delays. Are there any side effects from the new system which might warrant modification, or simply be a lesson that the project brief didn't look far enough?

- costs and benefits;

- user reaction;

- superseded jobs. Were any previous jobs found unnecessary since the introduction of the system?

- unplanned advantages. Have any unexpected benefits come out of the project?

6

PRINCE techniques

6.1 Planning steps

The general sequence of preparing a PRINCE plan follows this order:

What products are needed?

In what sequence should they be produced?

What activities will produce these products?

How long will the activities take?

When should they be done and by whom?

How much will that effort cost?

The method of planning recommended by the CCTA is based on thinking of the products to be produced during the plan timeframe. Not all of the steps are mandatory. PRINCE only insists on the Technical Plan, familiar to many as a bar chart, the Resource Plan and the Resource Plan Graphical Summary. Most of the project planning and control software on the market can produce these, although very few start from consideration of the products.

Figure 6.1 shows all the components of a PRINCE plan. This section takes you through each component and tries to show that a product-based approach is sensible and offers a simple, step-by-step method of planning. The explanation is based on a simple example.

Let's assume that I am a landscape gardener. A client has had a large house built and the garden is an acre of wilderness and rubble. The project is to clear the site, plant flower beds and lawns, build a patio and barbeque, put up a garden shed and buy a new set of garden tools for the client's use. The client has a reputation for being very fussy and hard to part from money.

6.1.1 Product Breakdown Structure

The first thing to do is write down all the products which will be created. It would be quite natural to begin by listing the major technical products. What is my ultimate product?

– finished garden.

What are the major products of which this will consist?

– purchased tools;

– stocked beds;

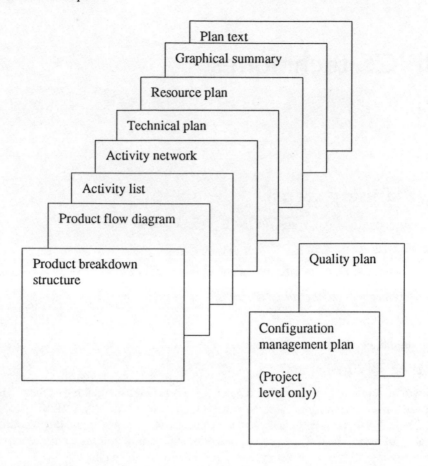

Figure 6.1 PRINCE plan components

- patio;

- lawn;

- barbeque;

- tool shed.

Will I have to create any extra products in order to produce these? Perhaps:

- agreed specification;

- approved design;

- cleared site;

- marked-out layout.

This is probably enough to give you the idea of generating the first part of the Product Breakdown Structure. Now PRINCE asks you to think not only of the technical products, but the management and quality products as well. Management products cover such things as the contract we would draw up, the plan itself, progress reports, acceptance criteria, confirmation in writing from the client that we have reached certain points satisfactorily, invoices and so on. Quality products include descriptions of all the technical products and their quality criteria, plus records which will demonstrate that quality checks are being carried out and any errors fixed.

The Product Breakdown Structure is a hierarchy of all these products under the three headings of management, technical and quality. Figure 6.2 shows a structure for our example. If it were a typical computer project, the Product Breakdown Structure at the project level might look like Figure 6.3. For a stage plan you would expect to see a lower level of detail. For example, if the first stage of the computer project were to be Initiation, then the Product Breakdown Structure for that would be similar to Figure 6.4.

6.1.2 Product Flow Diagram

The second step is to produce a diagram showing the sequence in which these products must be made and any interdependence between them. For instance, our picture should show that we would want to have an agreed specification and contract before doing any major work; the garden design should be done before laying the patio, and so on. Our diagram might look like Figure 6.5. It is often easier to put the ultimate product at the bottom of the page and work back from there.

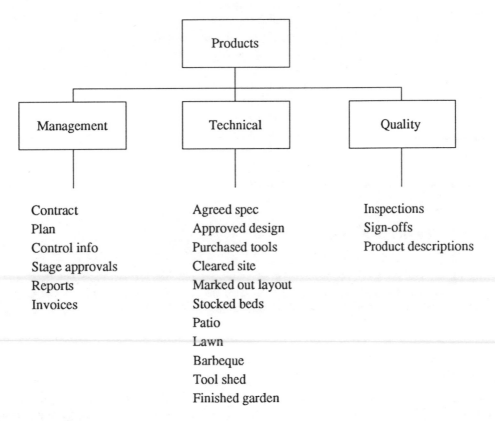

Figure 6.2 Garden project breakdown structure

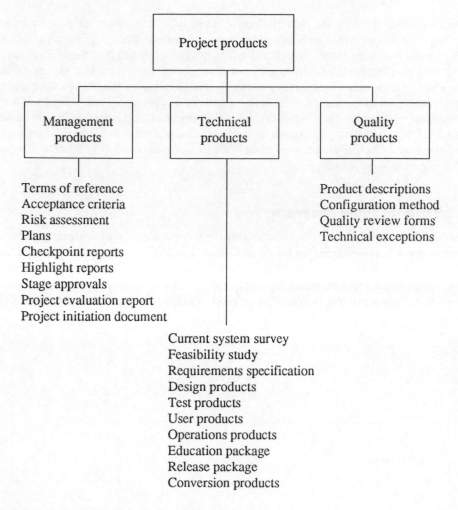

Terms of reference
Acceptance criteria
Risk assessment
Plans
Checkpoint reports
Highlight reports
Stage approvals
Project evaluation report
Project initiation document

Product descriptions
Configuration method
Quality review forms
Technical exceptions

Current system survey
Feasibility study
Requirements specification
Design products
Test products
User products
Operations products
Education package
Release package
Conversion products

Figure 6.3 Product breakdown structure for an IT project

6.1.3 Transformation

Having put our products into a sequence, we now need to think of the activities which will 'transform' one product into the next. These are written onto the Product Flow Diagram next to the relevant products so that they also are in sequence. Figure 6.6 shows this for our example and Figure 6.7 shows a Product Flow Diagram for the project level of a typical computer project.

6.1.4 Activity List

The activities are now listed in the order in which they occur and numbered, usually in increments of five or ten, just in case we need to insert one or two more later. To this list we add a duration column and write in there the estimated duration of each activity. Figure 6.8 shows an Activity List for our example.

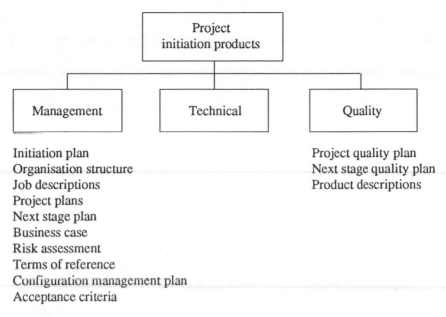

Figure 6.4 Project initiation product breakdown structure

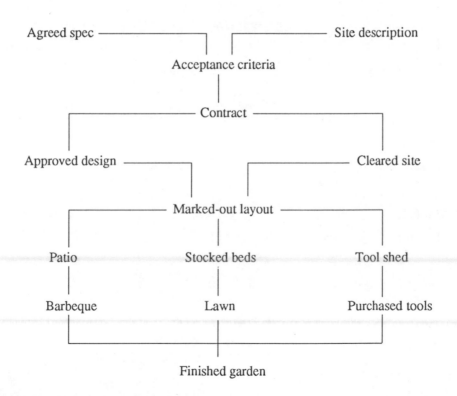

Figure 6.5 Garden project product flow diagram

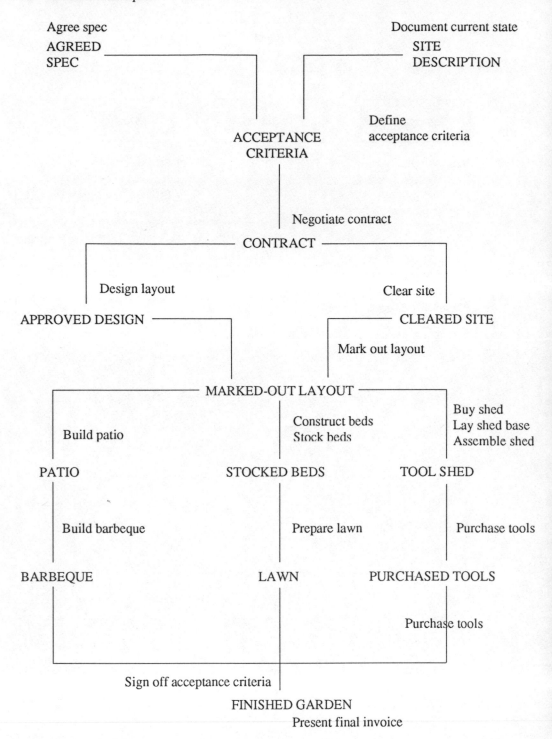

Figure 6.6   Garden product flow diagram plus activities

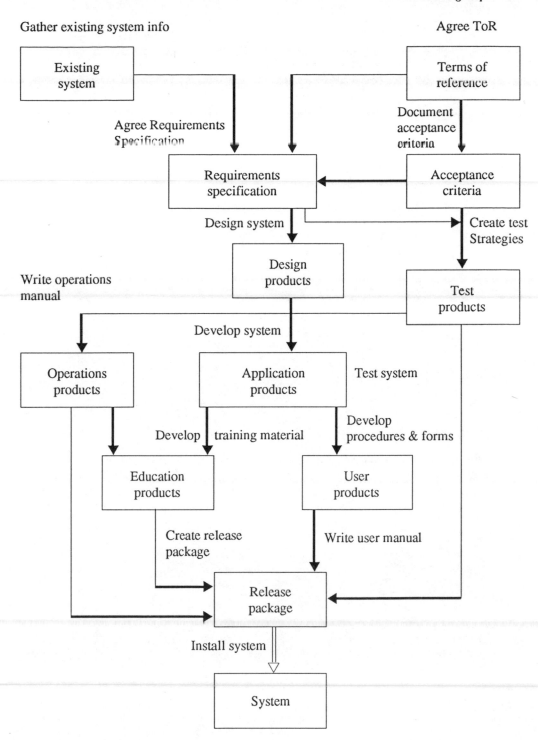

Figure 6.7   Product flow diagram plus activities

		Duration
10	Document current state	2
15	Agree spec	4
20	Define acceptance criteria	2
25	Negotiate contract	3
30	Design layout	8
35	Clear site	16
40	Mark out layout	4
45	Build patio	24
50	Construct beds	16
55	Stock beds	16
60	Buy shed	4
65	Lat shed base	8
70	Assemble shed	4
75	Purchase tools	2
80	Build barbeque	4
85	Prepare lawn	16
90	Sign off acceptance criteria	1
95	Present final invoice	1

Figure 6.8   Garden activity list

6.1.5   Activity Network

Using the information about sequence from the Product Flow Diagram and the expected durations from the Activity List, an Activity Network is produced. Figure 6.9 illustrates this for our example. Activity Networks are useful for showing sequence, dependencies, total duration, critical path and floats. All the planning and control software packages produce a network.

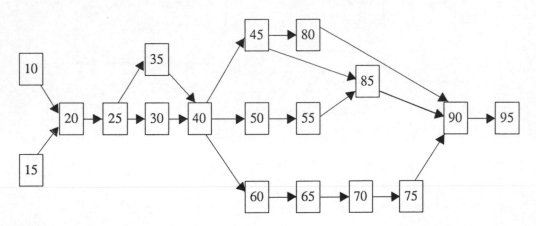

Figure 6.9   Activity network

6.1.6 Technical Plan

This is the PRINCE name for a bar or Gantt chart. Networks show a lot of information, but they are not good at answering questions such as 'Where will we be in June?', 'How heavily loaded is Mary in March?' or illustrating plan against actuals. The Technical Plan shows activities against a timeframe and is also the first planning step where we consider allocating activities to resources. Viewing the plan like this helps us to even out the resource utilisation within the sequence dependencies shown by the network. This plan is one of the mandatory ones in PRINCE. Figure 6.10 shows a Technical Plan for our example and assumes that we have three resources available.

6.1.7 Resource Plan

The next step is to turn this picture into a statement of the costs associated with the plan and summarise the resources needed. At a project level, the resources and costs would normally be accumulated by stage. At a stage level they would be accumulated by week or a similar period depending on the duration of the plan. Figure 6.11 is an example of a Resource Plan at project level.

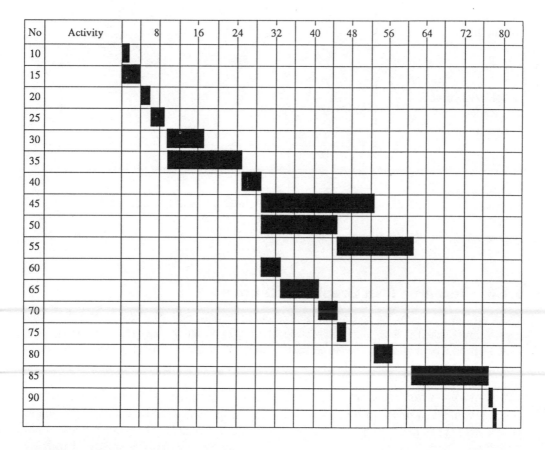

Figure 6.10   Technical plan

Effort	Stage 1	Stage 2	Stage 3	Stage 4
Systems analyst	12	8	6	4
Programmer	1	2	18	4
User	4	2	4	6
Operations	0	1	4	4
Admin	1	1	2	3
TOTAL EFFORT	18	14	34	21
Computer time			6 Hrs	75 Hrs

Costs	£k	£k	£k	£k
Systems analyst	72	48	36	24
Programmer	4	8	72	16
User	12	6	12	18
Operations	0	3	12	12
Admin	3	3	6	9
Total	91	68	138	79
Computer time			6	1
Consumables				4
Travel	2	1		4
Total	93	69	144	88
Cumulative	93	162	306	394

Figure 6.11   Project resource plan

6.1.8   Resource Plan Graphical Summary

These days, when reporting progress, management often demand a value analysis. Briefly this says, 'Don't just tell me how much has been spent against how much we expected to spend. Have I got the products which I expected to get for this money?' So they are looking for a graph which combines planned and actual costs with planned and actual delivery of products. PRINCE has a very simple graph for this. Figure 6.12 is a sample of how this form might look. The columns indicate the timeframe. In the project plan each column would be a stage. At the stage level each column would be a period of time such as a week. At the bottom of each column the major products due to be delivered during that period are listed vertically. The sample graph shows three rows of possible status for each product: is it available in draft form, has it passed a quality review, has it been handed over to the Configuration Librarian as ready? A tick is made in the

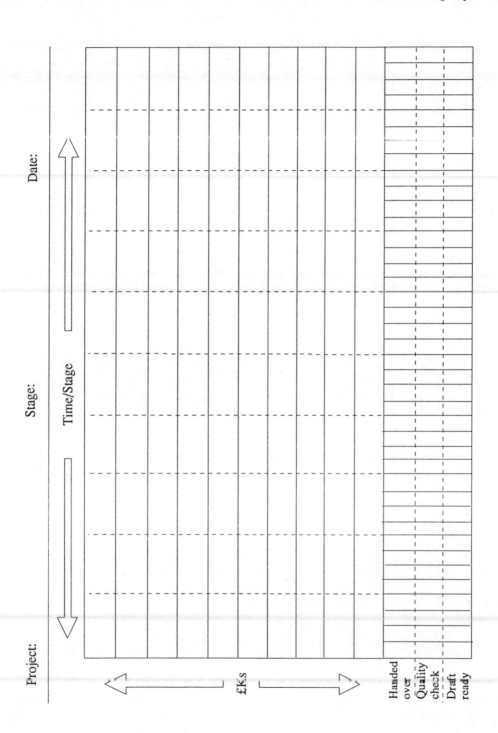

Figure 6.12 Resource graph

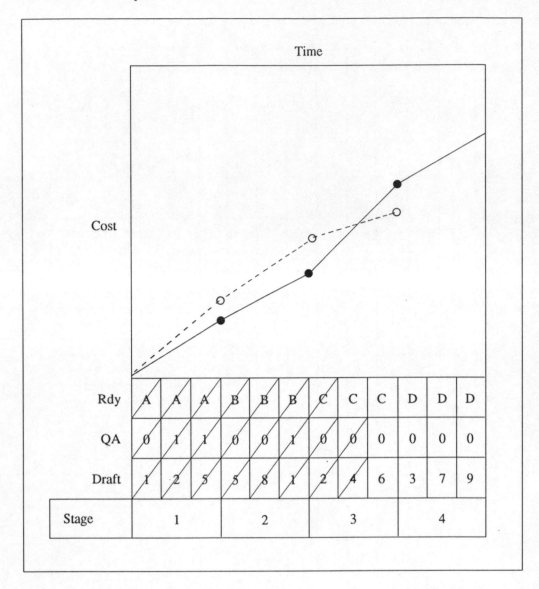

Figure 6.13 Project resource graph

appropriate box as the product moves through its lifecycle. Figure 6.13 is an example of a partially completed graph. Looking at it we can see that at the end of the first period all the products, A01, A12 and A15 are ready, but actual costs were a little higher than planned. A similar story exists after the second period. But at the end of the third period, although costs now appear lower than plan, the bottom of the graph shows a different story. Product C04 has been quality reviewed but is not yet ready, and product C06 has not even reached draft form. A look at the expected costs and times associated with finishing those products will probably show that the project is late and over budget.

6.1.9 Plan Text

Any of the aforementioned plans on their own would mean nothing – they need words to put them in context. In PRINCE the supporting text comes under five headings:

Plan description;

Assumptions;

External dependencies;

Plan pre-requisites;

Reporting.

6.1.10 Plan Description

This explains what the objective of the plan is and describes its environment under the headings:

Narrative summary;

Background;

Intended approach (bought-in or developed, what techniques);

Constraints or objectives affecting the plan;

Quality plan;

Configuration management plan (this is only required in a project level plan).

6.1.11 Assumptions

It is important to document any assumptions when making the plan. For example, the planner may be assuming a certain availability of a specific resource, or what the project priorities are. It is important for the Project Board to know this in their consideration of the plan. Is the assumption reasonable? Does a member of the Project Board have more information about the assumption? On a defensive note, if a plan is accepted and later on one of the documented assumptions is proved false, the responsibility is shared by the planner and those who accepted the plan.

6.1.12 External Dependencies

This identifies products coming from resources outside the control of the project manager, eg other suppliers, other systems. The intention here is to enlist the help of the Project Board if there are problems with these dependencies.

6.1.13 Plan Pre-requisites

Anything which must be in place before the planned activities can commence should be identified. Examples here might be facilities such as computer time or terminals, training for the stage team, access to areas or people, or information. These are items which will not be obvious from examination of the Technical Plan.

6.1.14   Reporting

This section details the methods, frequencies and formats of all reports to be made during the life of the plan. It covers written reports, updated plans and any face-to-face meetings. It should include the meetings of all levels, not only project manager to Project Board.

6.2   Quality review

6.2.1   Purpose and Benefits

The definition of a quality review is 'a team method of checking product quality'. This means that one or more people will be asked to check the correctness of a product developed by someone else. The major objective is to improve product quality, but there are side-benefits, such as:

- *Catching errors early*   Quality reviews can be held on any product and on completion of any step in a product's lifecycle. For example, the first chapter of the requirements definition could be reviewed while the other chapters were being written; a program design could be reviewed before the code is done. Catching errors as early as possible means saving money. It avoids later work being based on faulty data.

- *Monitoring the use of standards*   It doesn't need a very large team before it is impossible for the project manager to personally check that every piece of work is being done according to the required standards. The quality review method enables the checking to be spread around as many people as are necessary. The reporting mechanism within it ensures that the project manager is kept informed. It provides an ideal vehicle to keep the Technical and User Assurance Co-ordinators involved in the product development.

- *Improving status control*   It is one level of confidence for the project manager to be told by the developer that a product is finished. But it is much better to be told by independent reviewers that the product is ready and error-free.

- *Spreading product knowledge*   The involvement of other team members in quality reviews means that they get a good understanding of someone else's product. This is beneficial if their own work interfaces with the other product. Should the original developer then leave or be absent for any reason, one of the reviewers could pick it up without a large learning curve.

There are very formal procedures through which each review must pass. The generated documentation is filed and is an audit trail for anyone wishing to inspect the quality work being carried out.

The formal procedures have two parts. There are certain roles which must be allocated and each review must pass through three defined phases.

6.2.2 Quality Review Phases

The three phases are Preparation, Review and Follow Up.

6.2.2.1 Preparation

The objectives of this phase are to make the arrangements for the review and give the reviewers a chance to examine the product on their own, The activities are:

Decide the attendees.

Arrange the venue.

Distribute the product and invitation.

Reviewers examine the product and prepare question lists.

Based on the returned question lists an agenda is prepared.

Notify the Business Assurance Co-ordinator of any delay from the planned review date.

The length of time needed for this phase depends on such items as distribution delay, how much examination time is needed, how far the reviewers will have to travel for the review.

6.2.2.2 Review

The objectives are to agree a list of errors, if any, and allocate corrective actions. The activities are:

Chairman's opening remarks.

Presenter's overview, reasons for the particular approach.

Step through the reviewers' question lists.

Agree a corrective action list.

Allocate corrective work.

Decide who will approve each correction.

Agree on the review result.

Notify the quality file.

For reviews to be effective and staff to be tempted to come back next time, a review should be kept to a maximum of two hours. This means controlling the size of the product to be reviewed so that a thorough job can be done in this time, splitting up the product if need be.

6.2.2.3 Follow Up

The objective is to correct any identified errors. The activities are:

Correct errors.

Pass to which reviewer(s) were appointed to approve the corrections.

Distribute the signed off action list to all reviewers.

Notify the quality file.

6.2.3   Quality Review Roles

In summary the formal roles are:

The presenter, usually the author of the product to be reviewed.

The chairman, who controls the administration of the review.

One or more reviewers, who must study the product in advance and be prepared to comment on its correctness and completeness.

For the review of a major product there might be as many as six reviewers. More than that tends to get unwieldy. Most quality reviews will probably be informal ones. This means just two people getting together with one checking the work of the other. But even here not only must the three phases be used, all the roles must be allocated. In an informal review, the developer would play the role of presenter and the other person would be chairman and reviewer.

The Business Assurance Co-ordinator is responsible for co-ordinating all quality review work in a project and for filing the resulting documentation. Because of this the Business Assurance Co-ordinator may often sit in on reviews, sometimes taking the chairman's role.

The actual role responsibilities are as follows.

6.2.3.1   Chairman's Responsibilities

Preparation Phase

1   Check with the presenter that the product is ready for review.

2   If not, send an Exception Memo to the Business Assurance Co-ordinator with as much detail as possible, eg revised completion date.

3   Consult with the presenter and the Project Assurance Team to select appropriate reviewers.

4   Agree the amount of preparation time required with the presenter (and reviewers if this is appropriate).

5   Arrange a time, location and duration for the review in consultation with the presenter and reviewers.

6   Send an Exception Memo to the Business Assurance Co- ordinator if there is to be any delay in holding the review.

7   Arrange for copies of any relevant checklist or standard to be provided by the Technical Assurance Co-ordinator.

8   Ensure the Configuration Librarian provides product descriptions and product copies for all reviewers.

9 Send an invitation, product description, product copy, checklist and standard to each reviewer.

10 Send a copy of the invitation to the presenter and Business Assurance Co-ordinator, the latter for filing in the quality file.

11 Decide if a short overview presentation of the product to the reviewers is required prior to the review, and arrange it if it is.

12 Arrange with the reviewers for collection of a copy of their question lists prior to the review.

13 Create an agenda for the review from the question lists in consultation with the presenter. Prioritise the questions and roughly allocate time.

14 Confirm attendance with each reviewer shortly before the review.

15 If necessary, rehearse the review with the presenter.

Review

1 Provide a copy of the agenda to all attendees.

2 Open the review, stating objectives and apologising for any non-attendees.

3 Decide whether the reviewers present and the question lists from those unable to attend are adequate to review the product. If not, the review should be stopped, rescheduled and an Exception Memo sent to the Business Assurance Co-ordinator.

4 Invite the presenter to give a short overview of the product with no interruptions other than those necessary for clarity.

5 Step through the agenda with the appropriate reviewer enlarging where necessary on the question.

6 Allow reasonable discussion on each question between presenter and reviewers to decide if any action is required.

7 Document any agreed actions required on a Follow Up Action List.

8 Prevent any discussion of possible solutions or matters of style.

9 Ensure every reviewer is given the chance to voice their comments.

10 Where agreement cannot be reached on a point in a reasonable timeframe, declare it an action point and note the reviewer(s) concerned.

11 Where necessary, decide on the premature close of the review in the light of the comments made.

12 If faults are identified in products not under review, ensure that a Project Issue Report is raised and sent to the Configuration Librarian.

13 Collect any annotated product copies detailing minor or typographical errors.

14 Read back the Follow Up Action List and obtain confirmation from the presenter and reviewers that it is complete and correct.

15 Identify who is to be involved in working on each action item. Obtain a target date for completion of the work.

16 Agree with the reviewers who is to approve the work done on each action item and note this on the Follow Up Action List.

17 Pass the Follow Up Action List and all copies of the annotated product to the presenter. Lodge a copy of the Follow Up Action List with the Business Assurance Co-ordinator.

18 Decide with the reviewers what the status of the review is. It can be:

- complete with no errors discovered;

- complete with some rework required;

- in need of rework and another review.

19 Complete a Result Notification and distribute copies to all attendees and the Business Assurance Co-ordinator.

20 If the review is incomplete, forward the Follow Up Action List, Question Lists, annotated product copies and Result Notification to the Business Assurance Co-ordinator. Recommend a course of action to the project manager. The CCTA PRINCE manual offers five possible courses of action. The last two of these are not recommended:

- the product should be reworked prior to another review;

- the review should be reconvened to finish but with no interim need for rework;

- the review should be reconvened with no rework with a different set of reviewers;

- the review should be declared complete, the errors found so far corrected, and the rest of the product accepted as is;

- the review should be abandoned and the product used as is, ie none of the errors corrected but noted in a Project Issue Report.

Follow Up

1 Monitor the correction of errors and the signoff of the rework.

2 If an action cannot be taken within the time allowed, the chairman and presenter may decide to transfer it to a Project Issue Report, for referral to the Project Assurance Team as a possible off-specification. This requires the agreement of the project manager. The Follow Up Action List is updated with the Project Issue Report number and those waiting to sign off the item informed.

3 If the presenter requires more time than agreed to correct the action items, raise an Exception Memo and send copies of it to the presenter, reviewers and Business Assurance Co-ordinator.

4 On completion and sign off of all action items, sign off the Follow Up Action List as complete and pass it to the Business Assurance Co-ordinator with copies to all reviewers.

5 Supervise the passage of the error-free product to the Configuration Librarian.

6.2.3.2 Presenter's Responsibilities

Preparation

1 Ask the Business Assurance Co-ordinator to nominate a chairman if none is identified in the Technical Plan.

2 Confirm to the chairman that the product will be ready for review. This should occur several days prior to the planned review date to allow for preparation time.

3 Agree the attendees with the chairman and the Project Assurance Team.

4 Agree with the chairman and reviewers the length of the preparation and the location of the review.

5 Assess the Question Lists from the reviewers.

6 Agree the agenda with the chairman in the light of the Question Lists.

7 If required, arrange a short overview presentation to the reviewers prior to the review.

Review

1 Give a brief overview of the product, explaining:

– why it was produced and for whom;

– any assumptions made;

– the approach taken;

– the reasons for this approach.

2 Clarify any points about the product.

3 If the review is judged to be complete, collect from the chairman the Follow Up Action List and any annotated copies of the product from the reviewers.

Follow Up

1 Resolve all allocated action items.

2 Obtain sign-off for each action item from the nominated reviewers.

3 If an action item cannot be resolved within the time allowed, then the chairman and presenter may decide to transfer it to a Project Issue Report.

4 Inform the chairman if the resolution of the action items cannot be completed within the time allowed and agree new target dates.

5 Pass the Follow Up Action List to the chairman on resolution of all the action items.

6.2.3.3 Reviewer Responsibilities

Preparation

1 Consult the product description and any pertinent checklists and standards against which the product should be judged.

2 Allow sufficient time to prepare for the review.

3 Consult any necessary source documents from which the product is derived.

4 Annotate any spelling or typographical mistakes on the product copy, but do not add these to the Question List.

5 Check the product for completeness, defects, ambiguities, inconsistencies, lack of clarity or deviation from standards. Note any such items on the Question List.

6 Forward the Question List to the chairman in advance of the review. If possible, this should be done early enough to give the presenter time to digest the points and prepare an agenda with the chairman.

7 Forward a Question List and the annotated product copy to the chairman if unable to attend the review.

Review

1 Ensure that the points noted on the Question List are raised at the review.

2 Restrict comments to faults in the product under review.

3 Avoid attempting to re-design the product.

4 Avoid 'improvement' comments if the product meets requirements and standards.

5 Approve the Follow Up Action List as complete and correct when read back by the chairman.

6 Agree to assist in the resolution of any action items if requested by the chairman.

7 Request to check and sign off any action items either raised personally or which impact the reviewer's area of expertise or interest.

Follow Up

1 Work with the presenter to resolve any allocated action item.

2 Check and sign off those action items where they appear as reviewer.

6.2.3.4   Business Assurance Co-ordinator's Responsibilities

Preparation

1 Allocate a number to the quality review.

2 Select a chairman where none is identified in the stage plan.

3 Confirm that the review is to be held on time.

4 Amend the stage plan if the review is late. Raise an Exception Memo for this if the chairman has not already done so. Put details of any delay on the next Checkpoint Report.

5 File a copy of the quality review invitation in the quality file.

Review

 1 Act as reviewer or chairman if required.

 2 If requested by the chairman act as scribe for the action items.

Follow Up

 1 File the quality review result notification in the quality file.

 2 Update the Technical Plan appropriately.

 3 If the review were declared incomplete:

   – pass a copy of the quality review result notification, question lists, annotated products and the Follow Up Action List to the stage manager with the chairman's recommendation;

   – replace the quality review result notification with an updated one after the stage manager's decision;

   – circulate a copy of the quality review result notification, updated with the stage manager's decision, to the chairman, presenter and reviewers.

 4 File the Follow Up Action List when it has been signed off by the chairman as complete. Make a note of this for the next Checkpoint Report.

6.2.4   Exception Memo

This is a control document which does not receive a great deal of attention in the PRINCE manuals. Its use is to record exceptions from the planned quality review dates and activities. It is normally raised by the review chairman and sent to the Business Assurance Co-ordinator to amend the plan, but the stage manager or Business Assurance Co-ordinator can raise it.

An Exception Memo is raised if:

 – a product is incomplete when its quality review is due;

 – there is a problem during the preparation phase which means the review date will slip;

 – the review is declared incomplete.

It is used to update the Technical Plan, then filed by the Business Assurance Co-ordinator.

6.3   Configuration management

According to the CCTA, a configuration is a 'logically related set of products which need to be managed as a set.' It is the sum total of technical products to be produced by a specific project. It does not include the management and quality products. The PRINCE manual does suggest that the management products can be included, but this tends to obscure the real intention of configuration management.

The central purpose of configuration management is to have total control of those products which form part of the final system. That last phrase is the key. There are many technical products which will be developed on the way to producing the final system, such as the requirements specification and system test strategy. But they will not form part of the final system to be released. A Configuration Item is a product which forms part of the released system.

The management of these products means knowing which versions are the current ones, where they are, who is working on them and what their status is. Once they have passed a quality review, the products come under the control of the Configuration Librarian, who keeps the master and details of any copies issued.

There may be many versions of a product during its lifecycle. For example, the user may want a new feature and a program has to be changed to incorporate this. In this case it is easy to see that a new version will be created. But even while the product is being built there is a need to 'freeze' a product, and have everyone concerned agree on and approve the product in its current form so that it can be used as a firm basis for future work. In PRINCE, once a product version has been agreed and quality reviewed, it is 'frozen' and details taken of its linkage with other products and their versions. This is known as a baseline. When the complete system is to be released, the latest system baseline tells the librarian what versions of all the products need to be gathered together.

Let's clarify this with a simple example. A software house decides that it will create a new word processing package. The first Configuration Item which can be identified is the entire system, a word processing package. At the outset they don't know what the exact components will be. Later on they identify that the system will comprise the parts shown in Figure 6.14. The Configuration Librarian might use cards to keep track of the products. Card 1 would tell the librarian the latest system baseline number, the baseline numbers of the individual parts which comprise that system baseline number and point to cards 2, 3 and 4 for the contents. In turn these cards would point to lower level components until the actual programs, pieces of text, libraries, cardboard boxes, etc were reached. The librarian would then collect up all the lowest level components with the appropriate baseline number and assemble the release. This is just like a bill of material in manufacturing.

With a computer system, some of the products will be paper-based and others will be in machine-readable form. In the example above, there would be products such as the ring binder for the user manual, pre-printed disk labels, the box into which the entire system would be packed. The librarian must supervise libraries containing all types of product, have control over the issuing of version numbers, and have procedures available to move products into and out of these libraries. Let's have a look at the job of Configuration Management.

Configuration Management performs the following functions:

- identifying the individual products and types of product (eg machine-readable object modules) of the final system. These are referred to as Configuration Items (CIs);

- identifying those products which will be required in order to produce the Configuration Items (for example, pre-requisites to a module of coding are the source, a program design and before that a specification);

- establishing a coding system which will uniquely identify a product;

- identifying the 'owner' of a product, the person to whom creation or amendment of that product has been delegated;

- recording, monitoring and reporting on the current status of each product as it progresses through its own specific life-cycle;

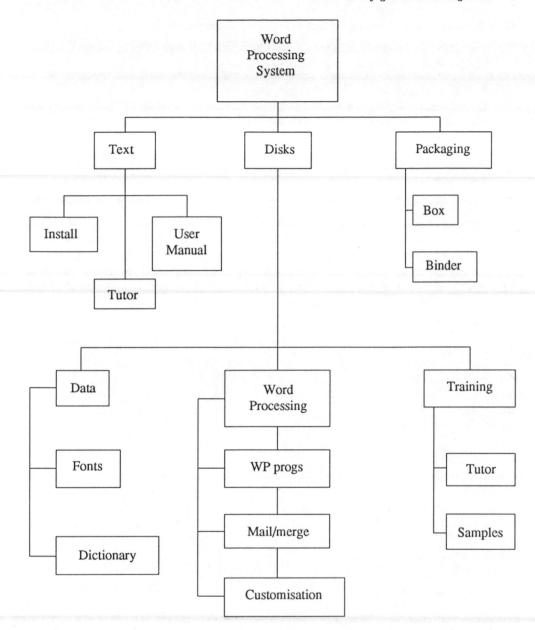

Figure 6.14 Configuration

- filing all documentation produced during the development life of the product;
- retention of master copies of every completed product within the Configuration Library;
- provision of procedures to ensure the safety and security of the products and control access to them;

- distributing and recording holders of copies of all products;

- maintenance of relationships between products so that no product is changed without being able to check for possible impact on its neighbours;

- managing change to all Configuration Items, from receipt of Requests for Change, through assessment of the impact of proposed changes, release of both human- and machine-readable copies of CIs to the eventual receipt of the amended versions;

- establishment of baselines;

- performance of configuration audits. This is a report comparing the status, actual version and baseline numbers of products with what the filing system says. It is very similar to a stock check, comparing what the card says is out there against what is actually there.

The point was made earlier that a Configuration Item is part of the final release of the system, but that there are many interim technical products which do not get released. These still need to be controlled. The best way is to bring them within the Configuration Management Method and use some key to differentiate between the products which form part of the release and those which don't.

Apart from the Configuration Management work the Librarian also creates and maintains the project and stage files.

Appendix 1
Form Samples

ACCEPTANCE CRITERIA

Project:	Date:	
Description	Measurement	Priority

OPERATIONAL COSTS

Project:							Date:	
Current system ☐ New system ☐								
	Yr 0	Yr 1	Yr 2	Yr 3	Yr 4	Yr 5	Total	
Hardware								
Rental or purchase								
Maintenance								
Teleprocessing								
Software								
Rental or purchase								
Maintenance								
Manpower								
User departments								
IT departments								
Other								
Administration								
Overheads								
Materials								
Stationery								
Consumables								
Data handling								
Data preparation								
Operations								
Miscellaneous								
Total Operating Cost								

COST/BENEFIT ANALYSIS

Project: Date:

	Yr 0	Yr 2	Yr 3	Yr 4	Yr 5	Yr 6	Total
Costs:							
Development							
Resources							
Other costs							
....							
....							
....							
Running costs							
Total costs							
Savings							
Current system							
Benefits							
....							
....							
....							
Total Benefits							
Cash flow							
Discount % DCF							

Net present value

RESOURCE GRAPH

Project: Stage: Date:

Time/Stage

£Ks

Handed over
Quality check
Draft ready

RISK MANAGEMENT CHECKLIST   Page 1

	Low Risk	Scale	High Risk	Weighting	Total
	Project Management				
1	Full time, experienced project manager	1 2 3 4	Inexperienced or part time project manager	(5–7) - - - -	- - -
2	User management experienced in projects and will participate effectively	1 2 3 4	Users inexperienced in projects with little participation expected	(4–6) - - -	- - -
	Project Staff				
3	Users expected to to be good quality actively involved with relevant knowledge of the system	1 2 3 4	Little user involvement and little relevant knowledge expected	(3–5) - - - -	- - -
4	High standard of supervision and narrow span of control	1 2 3 4	Span of supervision too wide and control level inadequate	(4–6) - - - -	- - -
5	The technical team is experienced of good quality and with appropriate skills	1 2 3 4	Inexperienced team lacking the needed skills	(2–4) - - - -	- - -
6	Staff are dedicated 100% of their time to the project	1 2 3 4	Staff have other work and are not 100% dedicated to the project	(3–5) - - -	- - -

RISK MANAGEMENT CHECKLIST Page 2

	Low Risk	Scale	High Risk	Weighting	Total
7	Low staff turnover	1 2 3 4	High staff turnover	(2–4) - - - -	- - -
	Project Description				
8	Staff are experienced in quality reviews and committed to their use	1 2 3 4	No quality reviews carried out in the past	(4–6) - - - -	- - -
9	Typical development cycle	1 2 3 4	Unaccustomed development cycle with no formal requirements definition	(2–4) - - - -	- - -
10	No unique or new hardware or software features	1 2 3 4	Pioneering new hardware or software features	(2–4) - - - -	- - -
11	Minimal impact on current operations	1 2 3 4	Significant impact on current operations	(3–5) - - - -	- - -
12	Hardware and software needs to be defined and documented to proven standards	1 2 3 4	Requirements not documented or not to proven standards; limited contingency margins	(2–4) - - - -	- - -
13	Little or no modification to existing application software	1 2 3 4	Extensive modification needed	(2 5)	

RISK MANAGEMENT CHECKLIST   Page3

	Low Risk	Scale	High Risk	Weighting	Total
14	Little or no other development work being done at the same time	1 2 3 4	Considerable other work competing for the same facilities	(2–5) - - - -	- - -
15	Little or no dependence on existing or developing systems not under the control of same staff	1 2 3 4	Dependent on systems or facilities not under the control of this project's staff	(3–6) - - - -	- - -
16	Project duration of one year or less, small number of work days	1 2 3 4	Duration more than one year; large number of work days	(2–4) - - - -	- - -
17	Little constraint on completion date apart from resource availibility	1 2 3 4	Mandatory and tight completion date	(3–5) - - - -	- - -
18	Plans and estimates based on reliable data and methods	1 2 3 4	Unreliable or non-existent planning data and methods	(3–6) - - - -	- - -
19	Business case made out based on reliable data and methods	1 2 3 4	No business case or one based on unreliable data or methods	(3–5) - - - -	- - -

RISK MANAGEMENT CHECKLIST Page 4

	Low Risk	Scale	High Risk	Weighting	Total
20	Suppliers are large, wel established companies	1 2 3 4	Suppliers are untried, new or not well financed	(2–4) - - - -	- - -
21	Few user departments	1 2 3 4	Several user departments	(4–6) - - - -	- - -
22	Few sites affected, easily accessible to the team	1 2 3 4	Many or remote sites	(3–5) - - - -	- - -
23	Minor impact on user's current or future work	1 2 3 4	Significant impact on user's work and methods	(3–5) - - - -	- - -
	Developer Maturity				
24	Well developed set of standards	1 2 3 4	Few standards no enforcement	(2–4) - - - -	- - -
25	Well defined quality policy		Ill defined quality policy	(3–5) - - - -	- - -
26	Clear delegation of authority	1 2 3 4	Centralised management with little delegation	(3–5) - - - -	- - -
27	Good relations with staff and unions	1 2 3 4	Poor staff and union relations	(2–4) - - - -	- - -

Business Risk Management Summary Sheet

(a) Sum of Total column   ☐

     Sum of Weighting column   ☐

(b) Weighting column x 2.6   ☐

(c) Weighting column x 2.0   ☐

Very high risk if (a) > (b)
Low risk if (a) < (c)

Business Risk Assessment:

Very high	☐
High	☐
Acceptable	☐
Low	☐

CHECKPOINT REPORT

Project: Stage:

Report Period From: To:

Achievements this period	By

Problems – Current or potential	For

Achievements next period	By

New Individual Work Plans required	By

HIGHLIGHT REPORT

Project: Stage:

Report Period From: To:

Signed:

Achievements this period

Problems – Current or potential

Achievements next period

END/MID-STAGE APPROVAL

Project: Stage:

Project Board signatures:	Role:	Name:
. . . .	. . . .	. . . .
. . . .	. . . .	. . . .
. . . .	. . . .	. . . .
. . . .	. . . .	. . . .
. . . .	. . . .	. . . .

Comments:

The project is approved to proceed to . . . . stage

Executive: Date:

TECHNICAL EXCEPTION LOG

Project:

No.	Date PIR raised	Author	CI affected	Technical exception type	Type change date	Allocated to	Date allocated	Date closed

PROJECT ISSUE

Project: PIR No:

Author: Date:

Situation Description

Appraisal

Affected CIs _____

Impact Description

Recommendation

Date: Appraised by:

Action   Date:

....

....

....

Closed ☐   RFC ☐   O-S ☐   Date:

REQUEST FOR CHANGE

Project: RFC No:

Date: From PIR No:

Requested by:

Description:

Reason & Benefits:

Required date:

Technical Evaluation:

Impact on project:

Cost:

Decision:

Authorisation: Date:

Role:

OFF-SPECIFICATION REPORT

Project: O-SR No:

Date: From PIR No:

Product affected:

Off-Specification Description:

Impact on project:

Impact analysis:

Cost:

First reviewed date:

Decision

      Allocated to. _ _ _ _ _ _ _ _   Date.

      De-scope   Date:

      Exception plan   Date:

      Deferred to later enhancement   Date:

QUALITY REVIEW INVITATION

Project   QR No:

To:

From:

Telephone:

You are invited to attend a Quality Review of:

Product: Configuration Identity:

Venue: Date:

Time: Duration:

Chairman:

Presenter:

Scribe:

Reviewers:

Attachments:			Useful references
Product ☐		Checklist	
Question list ☐		Standards	
		Other Products	

Please return a copy of your Question List to

not later than

QUALITY REVIEW QUESTION LIST

Project   QR No:

Product: Date:

Question No	Location	Description

QUALITY REVIEW ACTION LIST

Project:			QR No:	

Stage:			Date:	

Product:

Action no	Description	Action by	Target date	Checked by

Chairman's sign-off: Date:

QUALITY REVIEW RESULT NOTIFICATION

Project: QR No:

Product: Configuration Identity:

Result:

Completed	
Follow up by	
Re-scheduled	

Comments:

Chairman's signature   Date:

MEETING CHECKLIST

Subject: Date:

Venue: Time:

Expected duration:

Attendees:

Points to be raised:

Advance information required:

Items to be taken:

MEETING MINUTES

Subject: Date:

Attendees:

No	Minute	Action by	Target date

Appendix 2
Glossary

Acceptance Letters

There are five Acceptance Letters written during the final stages of a project:-

System Acceptance Letter is signed by the Senior Technical member of the Project Board on successful completion of the System Test. It may be prepared by the Stage or Project Manager.

Operations Acceptance Letter is prepared by the Operations Manager at each installed location of the system on confirmation that the product meets the Operations Acceptance Criteria.

User Acceptance Letter is signed by the Senior User member(s) of the Project Board when the system has passed the User Acceptance Tests and met the User Acceptance Criteria. It may be prepared by the Project or Stage Manager.

Business Acceptance Letter is prepared by the Executive of the Project Board at the end of the Project Closure meeting after confirmation that the other Acceptance Letters have all been signed.

Security Acceptance Letter is signed by the Executive at project closure to confirm that any security requirements have been met.

Activity Network

Puts all activities into a logical sequence, showing the dependencies and relationships between the activities. Given an estimate of the duration of each activity, the network shows the total time of the plan and provides a basis for scheduling the work to resources.

Approval to Proceed

Required from the Project Board at Project Initiation and each End-Stage Assessment in order that the project may proceed to the next stage. It represents a commitment by the Project Board members of the various resources identified in the Stage Plan.

83

BAC
See Business Assurance Co-ordinator.

Baseline
The 'freezing' of a product during the development of the system so that a known version of that product can be used either as part of a set of products to be released, or to form the firm base of a later product where it is needed as input. In order to be baselined a product must have successfully completed a Quality Review.

Business Acceptance Letter
A mandatory letter prepared by the Executive of the Project Board at the end of the Project Closure meeting after confirmation that the other Acceptance Letters have all been signed. It records the completion of the project against its objectives and is sent to the IT Steering Committee who instigated the project.

Business Assurance
The process of monitoring actual costs and time usage against the plans, signalling deviations and continual assurance that the Business Case of the project is not under threat.

Business Assurance Co-ordinator
A role within the Project Assurance Team responsible for planning, monitoring and reporting on all business assurance aspects of the project. The role also co-ordinates all Quality Review activities and often has overall responsibility for the Configuration Librarian's work.

Business Case
The justification for undertaking a project, defining the benefits which the project is expected to deliver, the savings it will bring judged against the costs of implementing the project and running the system.

Chairman
The person in charge of a Quality Review. Supervises the preparation phase, chairs the review. Keeps the momentum going during the review, prevents deviations, non-objective comments and stagnation on any point of disagreement. Ensures all actions are recorded and allocated.

Checkpoint
A technical control conducted on a regular basis relevant to the timeframe of the plan. The aim is to gather information on achievements and problems from a stage team, allow the team members to hear what other members are doing, disseminate external information to the team and report back in a written form to the Stage Manager. Normally led by the Team Leader with the

	Technical and Business Assurance Co-ordinators in attendance.
Checkpoint Report	Provides the information to update plans and create Highlight Reports by the Project Manager for the Project Board. If the roles are in use, it is produced by Stage Manager(s). If Stage Manager roles are not in use the reports are prepared by the Business Assurance Co-ordinator with help from the Technical Assurance Co-ordinator. If they have not attended the meeting the report is made out by the Team Leader.
CMM	*See* Configuration Management Method.
Configuration Librarian	A role with responsibility for administering Configuration Management, Technical Exception and filing procedures.
Configuration Management	The process of identifying and describing all the technical components created during the development of the system, controlling the status and change of those items, recording and reporting the status, and maintaining libraries of master copies of the items.
Configuration Management Method	A method for identifying all technical products, creating and maintaining libraries to hold the products plus the procedures to issue and receive the products and report on their status.
Control Points	PRINCE has four control points common to all stages:

    – End-Stage Assessment;

    – Mid-Stage Assessment;

    – Quality Review;

    – Checkpoint.

    See relevant entries in this glossary for more detail.

CRAMM	CCTA Security Risk Analysis and Management Methodology, a complete package which provides a structured and consistent basis to identify and justify all the protective measures necessary to ensure the security of IT systems.
Dependency	A constraint on the sequence and timing of work within a plan.

Detailed Resource Plan	Shows the resources and cost of a Detailed Technical Plan.
Detailed Technical Plan	A stage activity may be so complex or large that it merits a sub-plan all to itself to show the breakdown into small work units.
End-Stage Assessment	A mandatory management control at the end of each stage, consisting of a formal presentation to the Project Board by the Project Manager of the current project status and the proposed next stage plans. Signed approval by the Project Board is needed before the project can move into the next stage.
ESA	*See* End-Stage Assessment.
Exception Plan	Produced in situations where costs and/or timescale tolerances of a stage plan either have been exceeded or can be forecast to be exceeded. It is produced by the Project Manager and presented to the Project Board at a Mid-Stage Assessment.
Executive	A member (usually the Chairman) of the Project Board. The official reporting line to the IT Executive Committee. Specifically responsible for ensuring that the project achieves its expected benefits within its budget and schedule.
Highlight Report	Prepared by the Project Manager for the Project Board at intervals agreed with them when the stage plan was approved. It is based on the Checkpoint Report and covers new achievements, real or potential problems and a forecast of achievements over the next period.
Impact Analysis	The process of assessing the ramifications of a proposed change to the specification, listing what products would be affected by the change and evaluating the size and scope of change to each of the products.
Individual Work Plan	A definition of the tasks, responsibilities and performance measures of a team member, derived from the Stage Technical Plan and where relevant accompanied by a copy of the relevant Product Description.
Informal Review	A Quality Review carried out by two people, the person who created a product and a reviewer. The three phases of preparation, review and follow-up are still used, but

the normal roles will be shared. The presenter would also take the role of scribe, and the reviewer would also act as chairman. These often work best if kept to a review of 30 minutes or less.

IS	Information Systems.
IS Steering Committee	The top management group within a department responsible for the overall direction of the IS strategy. It may also be called the IT Strategy Committee.
IT	Information Technology.
IT Executive Committee	The senior management group responsible for overall direction of IT projects and implementation of the IT strategy. It initiates projects, appoints the Project Boards and sets Terms of Reference.
Library	A set of Configuration Items. These may be hardware, software or documentation.

Mid-Stage Assessment

A formal meeting between Project Board and Project Manager held for one or more of the following reasons:

– as an interim assessment of the progress of a long stage;

– to authorise limited work to begin on the next stage before the current stage is complete;

– to make a decision on an Exception Plan.

MSA	*See* Mid-Stage Assessment.
Off-Specification Report	Used to document any situation where the system fails to meet its specification in some respect. It is triggered by a Project Issue Report.
Operations Acceptance Letter	Prepared by the Operations Manager at each location where the system is installed after ensuring that the system complies with the Operations Acceptance Criteria.
PAT	*See* Project Assurance Team.
PBS	*See* Product Breakdown Structure.
PFD	*See* Product Flow Diagram.

PIR   *See* Project Issue Report.

Post Implementation Review   An integral part of the management and control of the project carried out six to twelve months after a system becomes operational. Its purpose is twofold; to check that the system has met its objectives and to check that the system is meeting user needs.

Presenter   At a Quality Review, usually the author of the item under review able to answer questions about the item in order to decide if there are errors or not.

PRINCE   PRojects IN Controlled Environments. The standard method of project management in government IT departments.

Product   Any final or interim output from a project.

Product Breakdown Structure   Identifies the products which must be produced. It is a hierarchical structure, decomposing the products through a number of levels with three main branches, representing technical, management and quality products.

Product Description   A description of the purpose, composition and quality criteria to be applied to the product. There should be a Product Description for every product.

Product Flow Diagram   Shows the required sequence of the development of the products and the dependencies between them.

Project   A project is regarded as having the following characteristics:

- a defined and unique set of technical products to meet a business need;

- a corresponding set of activities to construct those products;

- a defined amount of resources;

- a finite lifespan;

- an organisational structure with defined responsibilities.

Project Assurance Team   Consists of three technical and administrative roles, covering the whole project, and through whom project continuity and integrity are maintained. It comprises Business, Technical and User Assurance Co-ordinators.

Project Board	Consists of three management roles: Executive, Senior User and Senior Technical. One or more people may take each role depending on the interests of the project and the need to supply resources. It is necessary for the appointees to have managerial authority because of the need for them to make commitments.
Project Brief	*See* Terms of Reference.
Project Closure	The ending of the project requires formal approval and agreement from the Project Board. This may be combined with the End-Stage Assessment of the final stage.
Project Evaluation Review	A documented review of the project's performance, produced for the Project Closure. It ensures that any lessons learned are recorded for the benefit of other projects.
Project Initiation Document	Records the formal, business-like start to a project. It is prepared by the Project Manager and Project Assurance Team and approved by the Project Board. It contains:

– Terms of Reference;
– Acceptance Criteria;
– Project Organisation and responsibilities;
– Project Plans;
– First Stage Plans;
– Business Case;
– Business Risk Assessment;
– Product Descriptions.

Project Issue Report	Used as the initial document to raise any and all issues relating to the project apart from an action point from a Quality Review. If it requires action it will lead to either a Request for Change or an Off-Specification Report. If a point is raised during a Quality Review which is outside the scope of that review, it should be transferred to a Project Issue Report.
Project Resource Plan	Produced for the Project Initiation Document at the outset of a project, summarising the resources estimated to be required for the whole project, based on the Project Technical Plan.
Project Support Office	A central group of Configuration Librarians and Business Assurance Co-ordinators supplying those roles to a number of projects.

Project Technical Plan

Produced for the Project Initiation Document at the start of a project, showing the schedule of major activities for the whole project. It is an estimate.

PSO

See Project Support Office.

QA

See Quality Assurance.

Quality Assurance

The establishment of standards and procedures for quality control and the auditing, inspection and review of the procedures themselves, the quality controls carried out and the results obtained.

Quality Control

The examination and checking of products to ensure that they meet standards and their specification.

Quality Criteria

The characteristics of a product which determine whether it meets requirements, thus defining what 'quality' means for that product.

Quality Review

A procedure whereby a product is checked against an agreed set of quality criteria.

Request for Change

A means of proposing a change to the specification of the system. It can only be raised with the approval of the Project Manager after analysis of a Project Issue Report.

Reviewer

The role at a Quality Review which checks that a product meets its quality criteria.

RFC

See Request for Change.

Senior Technical

One of the roles on the Project Board representing the interests of the development resources. In addition the role represents the interests of technical management.

Senior User

A role on the Project Board representing the interests of the affected user community.

Stage

The PRINCE method allows a project to be divided into a number of stages. A stage represents either the amount of work which the Project Manager is confident about planning or how far the Project Board want the project to go before formally checking its progress and viability. The end of a stage is chosen to correspond with the completion of one or more major products.

Stage Manager	The manager of a stage, reporting to the Project Manager; this role may or may not be used.
Stage Resource Plan	A summary of the resource and cost needs of a stage, based on the Stage Technical Plan.
Stage Team	A composition of the skills needed to develop the products of a particular stage.
Stage Technical Plan	A chart of the technical, management and quality activities of a stage shown against an appropriate timeframe.
System Acceptance Letter	Prepared by the Project or Stage Manager for signature by the Senior Technical member of the Project Board confirming that the System Acceptance Tests have been successfully passed.
TAC	*See* Technical Assurance Co-ordinator.
Technical Assurance	The process of monitoring the technical integrity of products.
Technical Assurance Co-ordinator	One of the roles within the Project Assurance Team, responsible for defining technical standards for the various products, then planning, monitoring, advising and reporting on all technical aspects.
Technical Exception	An unplanned situation relating to one or more end products handled initially by creating a Project Issue Report which may lead to a Request For Change or Off-Specification Report.
Terms of Reference	A definition of the objectives for a project, its background, reasons and the constraints on a solution.
Tolerance	The permitted limits above and below a plan's budget and schedule. The Project or Stage Manager has freedom to operate within these limits, but must consult with the Project Board before continuing outside the tolerance level. The tolerance is agreed between Project Manager and Project Board on approval of the plan. At a project level the tolerance may have been passed down to the Project Board by the IT Executive Committee.
Transformation	The process of examining the Product Flow Diagram and defining what activities are required to create one product from its predecessors.

UAC	*See* User Assurance Co-ordinator.
User Acceptance Letter	A letter signed by the Senior User(s) on the Project Board after User Acceptance Tests confirming that the system meets the User Acceptance Criteria.
User Assurance	Protection of the user's interests in a project, ensuring that a full specification of its needs are obtained and that further project work continues to meet that specification.
User Assurance Co-ordinator	A role within the Project Assurance Team responsible for monitoring, advising and reporting on all user aspects of the project; a day-to-day representation of the user on the project.

Index